SURFING
the fundamentals

SURFING
the fundamentals

Jeff Toghill

Foreword by Barton Lynch

NEW HOLLAND

The author wishes to thank the following people who helped put this book together: Matt Grainer, principal of Manly Surf School; Marc Atkinson, surfing coach and proprietor of Dripping Wet Surf Co.; Geoff McCoy, one of Australia's top board designers and shapers; Matt Toghill, the author's son and one of Australia's new breed of surfers; Mark Donaldson, Manly photographer and surfer; Georgina Gifford, professional photographer and surfer; and the many other surfers, dealers and manufacturers who have made small, but significant, contributions.

First published in Australia in 1998 by
New Holland Publishers (Australia) Pty Ltd
Sydney • Auckland • London • Cape Town

14 Aquatic Drive Frenchs Forest NSW 2086 Australia
1A/218 Lake Road Northcote Auckland New Zealand
24 Nutford Place London W1H 6DQ United Kingdom
80 McKenzie Street Cape Town 8001 South Africa

National Library of Australia
Cataloguing-in-publication data:

Toghill, Jeff, 1932–
Surfing: the fundamentals
Includes index

ISBN: 1 86436 426 2.

1. Surfing. 2. Surfing – Australia. 3. Surfing – New Zealand. I. Title

797.32

Publishing General Manager: Jane Hazell
Publisher: Averill Chase
Editor: Julie Nekich
Designer: Andrew Cunningham
Artwork: Guy Holt
Typesetter: Melbourne Media Services
Printer: McPherson's Printing Group, Australia

CONTENTS

FOREWORD
by Barton Lynch

Few sports can induce the adrenaline rush that comes when riding down the face of a wave. Few sports can offer the stimulating excitement of challenging the elements in their most temperamental form. And few sports have the universal appeal to all ages, from the very young to the not-so-young. But then surfing isn't just a sport — it's a total lifestyle.

Since the days when Duke Kahanamoku first rode his big board in the waves off Freshwater beach, surfing has been a part of everyday life for most Australians and New Zealanders. Kids race out of school to beat their mates into the surf. Yuppies park their BMWs at the beach and unload their Mals, while more and more girls are taking to the water. Surfing has truly become a family-oriented activity. With a perfect climate, fantastic beaches and the big ocean swells, it's small wonder that surfers from this part of the world are among the elite of the international surfing scene.

But despite such popularity, surfing gets little recognition and even less support from government and corporate bodies (with a few notable exceptions). When I began surfing there was nowhere to learn to surf; no books on the subject and no organised surfing in schools. I remember my joy when we formed the first Mosman High Surfing Club. Nowadays, things haven't improved very much. A few surfing schools have started up and some of the pros are lending their time to teach youngsters, but still there is no assistance from official sources to help our young surfers climb the international surfing ladder.

That's why I'm pleased to see a book like this appear on a market where there have been few publications on surfing. Our surfers have always been among the world leaders in the sport, and to maintain this status we need a dedicated new breed of young surfers. This book will encourage newcomers to give it a try and help those who are already surfing to develop their skills. I hope you enjoy this book, and always remember that the best surfer is not the person who is surfing the best but the one with the biggest smile on his or her face.

INTRODUCTION

Like any sport, surfing looks easy when it's done by experts. The ease with which a good board-rider catches a wave, jumps up on the board and glides gracefully up and down the face, performing fantastic twists and turns like a waterborne ballet dancer, makes it all look so simple. Arms and legs co-ordinate as the surfer just keeps a hair's breadth ahead of the break and treats the wave with contempt, cutting back off the top and throwing a fan of white spray high into the air. Or racing through the barrel, thumbing his nose as he spits out the end just before it closes out in an angry boil of white water.

It looks easy but it's not—far from it. The pro surfer's graceful ease comes with years of hard training and many more years of experience. Surfing is very demanding and the sea is always an unforgiving mistress. Training, discipline and experience are all important factors in surfing, just as they are in any sport, and a lack of any one of these can lead at least to a smashed board, at worst to serious injury.

Surfing is a sport for girls as well as guys.

Danger is always lurking out there in the surf. Not in the form of sharks or rips—they are the lesser perils. The main threat lies in the waves themselves; in the sea which often looks so harmless but which can so quickly turn a simple mistake into a major disaster. There is only one way to counter this and that is to learn to surf the right way. A bike rider who doesn't learn to ride properly will fall off and get hurt. A horse rider who doesn't learn the right way to handle a horse is likely to be thrown. Skiers who don't learn the correct downhill drills will most certainly come a cropper at some stage. It is the same with surfing. If you don't learn how to ride your board correctly you will not enjoy surfing and may put yourself in serious danger. Learning about the waves is equally as important. If you don't learn about the sea sooner or later it will catch up with you and you will be very, very sorry.

Like sailors, surfers soon learn to respect the sea and to be prepared for what it may do. You won't see an experienced surfer just run down the beach, throw his board into the water and paddle out. He will stop and sit on the beach for some time, studying the waves' every move. There are signs that can tell you so much about what is happening out there and no surfer worth his salt will ignore them. They tell where the rips, banks and dangers lie and, of course, where the best waves are located. Ten or fifteen minutes on the beach studying the waves will pay great dividends when you get out there and start surfing—not just in terms of avoiding danger, but also in terms of improving your surfing.

That's just one aspect of learning the fundamentals of surfing. Once you leave the beach and paddle out to the break there are many more basic factors you must learn if you are to surf safely and get pleasure from your surfing.

And that's what this book is all about: learning the fundamentals of surfing. For surfers it is not just a sport, it's a way of life, and it must be grasped from the bottom up; from the simplest basics of picking the right board to make your surfing easy and pleasurable. No matter how good the waves, you can't surf without the right board, and no matter how good your board, you can't surf unless you know how to handle the waves. This book takes you step by step through all the basics of surfing. It won't make you a pro surfer, but it will get you off to a good start. You will learn how to surf safely and well—and that means you will get great pleasure as well as a sense of achievement from your surfing.

Where it all began

Surfing is a relatively recent sport compared with most. The traditional Roman and Greek athletes had no reason to think of surf as a sport medium because they lived on the Mediterranean Sea where there is no ocean swell. The west coasts of Britain and France face the Atlantic Ocean and have big swells, but the water was probably too cold to encourage any brave souls to put even their toes in. Those were the days before wetsuits!

Surfing as we know it today really began in the islands of the Pacific around the beginning of the twentieth century. The tiny nations not only face the open ocean, they are surrounded by it. It is small wonder then, that one day some local adventurer decided to ride a wave and found it was fun. The Hawaiians are recognised as the first to develop modern surfing, although their boards and techniques were far removed from those in use today.

The first island surfers carved their wooden boards from trees. Four to five metres long and heavy, these were known as 'guns'. Flat and with no refinements such as fins, the boards were controlled by the riders moving their feet along them and shifting their weight to change the attitude of the board to the wave. The thrill and excitement soon caught on and, before long, all the young Hawaiians were struggling down to the beach with their big, weighty boards and throwing them into the sea.

As new surfers developed their skills they began to challenge one another to prove who was best at the sport. Contests followed, champions were hailed, and the sport of surfing was born. It quickly spread across the world to Australia, New Zealand, California and South Africa, where surf and climate conditions are ideal and, before long, it had developed to become the international sport it is today.

The shape of boards has changed considerably over the years.

SURF SAFELY
a few basic tips

Don't surf by yourself … Always surf with a buddy or in waves where there are other surfers around. Or get someone to watch you from the beach. Simple things like leg cramp can become a major problem if there is no-one around to help you. A bang on the head from your board could cause you to drown if you're on your own, but if there is someone there to pull you out you'll only get a headache.

If you get dumped … Don't panic; stay calm and relaxed. Panicking can result in you swimming down instead of up, and frantically clawing for the surface uses breath and energy and shortens your survival time. Sooner or later the wave will let go and you can swim up to the surface. Open your eyes under water so you can see which way is up!

Watch the rips … They can be helpful but they can also be dangerous. If you find yourself caught, stay calm and paddle across it. Never try to paddle against it, even if the beach seems to be getting farther away. Even bad rips come to an end, and you can then paddle back to the break.

Scared? … Everyone is at some time. If a wave looks too big just ditch your board and dive under the wave. A big set is usually followed by a series of smaller waves so you can get back into the action when the big ones pass. Once again, stay calm.

Watch other surfers … Especially the good ones. You will not only learn a lot about riding your board but you will get to know where the best waves are.

Don't surf after dark ... Or even at dusk. If you have a nasty wipeout and get hurt no-one will see, so no-one will come to help you. Apart from that, noahs are on the prowl for their dinner after dark!

Get the right leg rope ... Too long and it will get caught round your neck and choke you. Too short and it will jerk the board back onto your head (see page 20 in this book).

Don't get cold ... You need to wear the right wetsuit for the conditions. Hypothermia can be a killer and it creeps up on you without warning. Get out of the water and change your wetsuit before cold turns to chill.

Can't paddle out? ... It's always hard work for a beginner. Watch where other surfers are paddling out and read the waves as they do. Practise your duck-diving techniques (see page 61 in this book). If a big wave is about to break on you, don't try to dive under it; turn and run back to the beach, it will lessen the impact.

Only by learning to surf correctly can you really enjoy the thrills.

ALL ABOUT
SURFBOARDS

Surfboards, like golf clubs, come in a wide range of shapes and sizes. Watch the board-riders on a popular surfing beach any day when the waves are reasonable and you will see long boards, short boards, thick boards, thin boards and boards with a variety of shapes and curves. If you examine them closely you will find that each type of board has specific characteristics—some have pointed noses, some round noses; there will be a variety of tail shapes such as pintails and swallow tails and a mixture of single fins, two fins or three fins. Some will be relatively flat along their length and some will curve excitingly up at the nose.

Such a diversity of boards can confuse the beginner but, just as with golf clubs, there is a reason for the many shapes and sizes and part of becoming an accomplished surfer lies with choosing the right equipment.

So how does a beginner know what to buy to ensure that he or she has the right board? In the next chapter we talk about discovering which board will suit you according to your bodyweight, your degree of expertise and the type of surfing you want to do. But first let's get to know what surfboards are all about so that when you go to a dealer, you will be able to understand what he is talking about.

Board types

The early Hawaiian boards were too big and heavy to be used by anyone but experts. Thankfully, modern boards are generally much shorter, lighter and more manoeuvrable. There are still many surfers who prefer long boards, so the range is quite extensive, and today even the long boards are mostly made of material that is considerably lighter and more durable.

Mals
When the sport caught on in places such as California, Australia and South Africa where the waves can still be big—although nothing like the waves in Hawaii—the length and shape of the board began to change. These boards, which were still quite long, were

Mals are more stable than short boards.

ridden in much the same way as the original Hawaiian tree planks and became known as 'Malibu' boards, after the popular coastal region on the Californian coast. There is still quite a strong following for 'Mals', and on most surfing beaches you will find Malibu boards mixing it with the shorter varieties.

Mini-Mals

These are really a compromise: they are not as long as Mal boards but are made in much the same style. They are a little longer than short boards, and are not shaped as drastically as performance boards. They are a useful board for beginners because they offer much of the stability of the Mal but have more manoeuvrability.

Short boards

Most surfboards in use today, especially those used for high performance, fall into the category known as short boards. This is something of a misnomer as they can be very short—down to 5ft 6in—but come in a variety of shapes, and lengths of up to almost a mini-Mal. As a rule short boards, no matter what the length, are shaped much more severely than a Mal in order to give them greater performance, and experienced surfers usually have custom-built boards made specifically for them to suit their style of surfing. For beginners, a moderate length board (7–8ft) is probably best to learn on because it offers a reasonably stable platform on which to get your balance, yet as you develop your skills it enables you to try out some of the more advanced techniques.

Guns

A gun—named after the big original boards used for surfing in Hawaii—is just a large board intended for use in big waves. Generally speaking, the smaller the wave the shorter the board, and guns are at the top end of the short-board scale, so they can cope with bigger waves. They are not mini-Mals, they are just a larger version of a short board. Despite their length and increased buoyancy, they are probably not the best type of board for beginners to learn on because their design, which is highly sophisticated, is meant for performance surfing and they will not have the stability of the mini-Mal.

How a surfboard is made

Modern surfboards are made from synthetic materials, which are much lighter than the timber or plywood used in early boards. Even the relatively long and bulky Mals are now light enough to be easily carried down the beach without giving yourself a hernia, while the short performance boards weigh little more than the proverbial feather.

Basically all modern surfboards consist of plastic foam in the form of a 'blank', a nondescript block, which is strengthened by inserting a timber spine or spines known as 'stringers', and shaped to the required dimensions and curves. The shaped blank is then covered with a coat of woven fibreglass onto which is poured a chemical resin. This is spread across and around the board before it sets to a hard surface, thus encasing the blank in a strong, durable and waterproof coating.

The blank
The blank is a block of plastic foam usually bigger than the planned surfboard. This enables the shaper to whittle away the extraneous foam until he gradually reaches the shape he requires—rather like a sculptor reducing a block of stone to a recognisable statue. This is the stage in the development of the board that will most influence its performance, as each shaper uses his individual skills to create a board for its intended use or to suit the specific surfer for which it has been designed.

Stringers
These provide the longitudinal, or lengthways, strength of the board. Stringers are most commonly full-length strips of timber.

Top surfboard designer Geoff McCoy painstakingly shapes a new custom board.

The most expensive and toughest material used for stringers is carbon fibre, the same sort of material that is used in high-performance yachts and in some types of aircraft manufacture. Most boards have one full-length stringer but it is not uncommon to have up to three stringers, particularly in long boards which are subject to great longitudinal stresses when in use.

The stringers are inserted into the foam of the blank and shaped so that they are flush with the surface—although they are usually quite visible in the finished product.

Shaping

As modern manufacturing methods influence the surfboard industry, more and more boards are being made by computer-controlled machines. These machines, which shape the blank to a specified design and shape, are controlled by a software program run through a computer which is hooked to the shaping machine. Surfboards made this way can be stock boards for general use or special custom-built boards for expert surfers. In the latter case the designer feeds his design into the computer, or even designs the board in the computer, and then runs the computer program to produce the board. Machine-shaped blanks are usually finished by hand, and custom-built boards would certainly be hand-finished by the designer or shaper himself.

The shaper uses a number of different tools to carve his design from the foam blank. Perhaps his most useful tool is a plane—usually an electric plane to form the initial shape, then a surform plane for the finer work. Other aids such as sanders, sanding blocks and gauze are used for finishing the shaped blank. Each shaper has his favourite tools to make his work easy and to enable him to create a board that will offer high performance for its owner.

Glassing

When the blank has been sanded to its final shape it is ready for the hard coat that will protect it when in use. This is done by wrapping woven fibreglass cloth around the foam blank and saturating it with a resin—usually an epoxy resin. The resin impregnates the fibreglass and secures it to the blank. As the resin sets, it creates a thin but very strong skin which is totally waterproof and which is bonded to the shaped blank to complete a very lightweight but strong unit. Different weights of glass fibre cloth can be used to vary the thickness and strength of the finished board.

A lucky surfer with his custom-built board.

Finishing

There are many finishes which can be used to enhance the appearance of the board before it goes into the showroom. Some manufacturers give it a high-gloss finish, others a matt or satin surface. There is no specific performance advantage of either, although some surfers prefer one over another for personal reasons. Colours and logos are incorporated in the glassing stage of manufacture, as are fins and leg-rope plugs. Depending on the number of fins required as well as the choice of fin sizes and shapes, the manufacturer will fit each board individually and then, in most cases, glass the fins into place. Some fins can be fitted into sockets or boxes of a board so that they can be changed—a personal preference for some surfers.

Parts of a surfboard

Names used for the parts of a surfboard can vary around the world, but the most common terms are those given below:

Nose
This is the front tip of the board, which is often pointed but may be rounded, especially in larger boards such as Mals. Because of the potential danger of a sharply pointed nose to other surfers, a plastic cone or nose guard is often fitted.

Tail
This is the back or rear end of the board. This may come in a number of different shapes, all of which are designed to give certain performance characteristics to the board under specific conditions. Since the surfer's rear foot is placed close to the tail and is a major factor in manoeuvring the board, different shaped tails effect the response of boards to some of the powerful surfing techniques. Many pro surfers have their own ideas about the shape of the tail on their board, depending on how it affects their surfing. There are many versions of the tail design—one is the 'posh' tail, a combination of round pin and squash! Such tails are mostly individual creations by shapers and designers and are aimed at improving the performance of a board.

Rocker
This is the term given to the upwards curve of the board along its length. It plays an important part in the board's response to turns and other tight manoeuvres.

Deck
The top of the surfboard, like that of a boat, is called the deck. Also like a boat, it's the part you stand on. The deck of a new board is very slippery so wax or grip must be used to prevent your feet slipping off when the board is wet.

Rails

This is the term given to the sides of the board where they curve over from the deck to the bottom. Most surfers grab the rails to help them jump to their feet when the board takes off on the top of a wave. Also leaning or 'edging' the rails into a curve can assist in turning the board in tight manoeuvres.

Fin

The fin is the protrusion under the tail of the board. Modern surfboards may have one, two or three fins and they can come in different shapes and sizes depending on the needs of the surfer or the design of the manufacturer. The difference lies mostly in the performance of the board: a single fin is best for good sweeping turns whereas for tight cut-backs or re-entries twin fins are generally better. Most short boards these days have two fins.

Leg-rope plug

This is a small socket indented into the deck of the board close to the tail with some form of securing device into which the end of the leg rope is fitted.

Ancillary gear

The sort of ancillary gear required to start surfing can vary according to location, climate and the requirements of each surfer. Basically, the following equipment is essential in order to begin serious surfing in temperate climates:

Wetsuit

Modern wetsuits are highly technical and can range from basic singlet tops for use in tropical climates to full-covering wetsuits which can be used in even the coldest winters. They are made mostly from neoprene or rubber and the main types of wetsuits in use these days fall into one of the following categories:

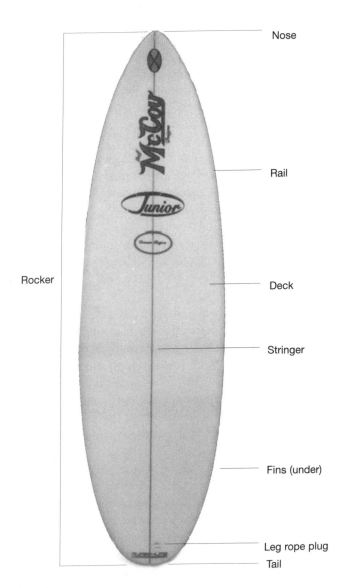

Nose

Rail

Rocker

Deck

Stringer

Fins (under)

Leg rope plug

Tail

Parts of a surfboard.

Steamer: A full wetsuit with long sleeves and long pants designed for cold conditions. Usually made of 3mm neoprene (or thicker, for colder climates).

Short-sleeved steamer: Designed for less rigorous conditions, such as cold to temperate climates, these are usually made up of 2 or 3mm wetsuit material which gives good body warmth but allows more freedom for the arms.

Spring suit: Short sleeves and short legs designed for most temperate conditions and made from material around 2mm in thickness. These are ideal summer wetsuits, for conditions where the water or air never gets too cold.

Singlet top: A sleeveless top with long or short pants made from 1.5 or 2mm neoprene. These are well suited to warm or hot climates.

Rashie

This is an anti-rash 'T-shirt', usually made of lycra and worn under a wetsuit. It prevents the wetsuit material chafing your skin by allowing it to move more freely over your body. Rashies are worn 'inside out' (the seams on the outside for maximum protection to the skin) and are mostly made from anti-UV material so that when it's too hot to wear a wetsuit, you can still wear your rashie for protection from the damaging rays of the sun.

Helmet

Coming more and more into use, helmets are usually worn in bad conditions or when surfing a dangerous break. Even professionals wear helmets when surfing over coral or rock. Standard helmets encompass the whole head and are similar to those worn by motorcyclists, though perhaps not so bulky. More expensive helmets have sun visors made from polaroid perspex to help cut the glare of the sun reflecting off the waves.

The type of wetsuit you need depends on the weather. This is a short-sleeved steamer.

Leg rope

A very important part of a surfer's gear, leg ropes can mean the difference between keeping your board with you and having to swim a long way home. Leg ropes come in many lengths and thicknesses and it is important to get advice from an expert in choosing the most suitable for your board and for the likely surf conditions. Leg ropes can be dangerous and beginners should start by using a fairly long rope. A short rope can pull the board up quickly in a wipeout and catapult it back against your head or body, inflicting a nasty blow. The long rope keeps a safe distance between you and the board. However, care is also needed with a long leg rope, because a long, trailing rope can snag around rocks or coral or, in a wipeout, tangle around your neck or arms as you fight to get out of the swirling surf.

Wax

For many years wax was the only substance used to provide a grip on the slippery deck of the board and it is still widely used today. It is sold in convenient packages and every surfer should include it in his gear. Also important is a wax comb, used to 'rough up' the wax when it becomes smooth with use and to provide a better footing, or to scrape off old wax prior to rewaxing.

Grip

This has replaced wax in many cases. It comes in many shapes and sizes, the most common being the rubber or composite tread used at the rear of the deck for the back foot. Grip in the middle of the board is sometimes used for the front foot. As far as performance is concerned, the choice between grip and wax is a personal one although the traditional wax has never lost its popularity with pro surfers.

Booties

Booties are not generally favoured by most surfers as the feel of the board is lost when the foot is encased in the bootie material

A rashie prevents wetsuit chafing, and is a good anti-UV shirt when worn on its own.

(usually neoprene). However, they can be a godsend when you have to walk out to the water across sharp rocks or coral or when the water is freezing!

Nose guard

As mentioned earlier, nose guards are plastic fittings glued over the pointed nose of some surfboards to protect that part of the board and to reduce the risk of serious injury if the board strikes someone in the water. They are cheap and easy to fit and should be used on all boards with a pointed nose.

Repair kit

It is almost impossible to surf seriously without, at some stage, suffering 'dings' or scratches to the board. A big wave can damage a board as a result of striking another board or by hitting the bottom. Big seas can easily snap a surfboard in half, although that situation calls for more than just a temporary repair!

A repair kit with resin, fibreglass and wet and dry sandpaper is sufficient to take care of minor dings and scratches. The board will need to be totally dry before you apply any resin, so repairing dings is usually an overnight job. To continue surfing until you have time to do a proper repair job, keep a roll of commercial-grade insulating tape in your repair kit. Bad dings need a professional repair job, or the strength and structure of the board can be affected. Your dealer will usually take care of those.

Grip is mostly used to give the back foot a firm hold.

BUYING THE RIGHT SURFBOARD

Now that you have some idea about surfboards and surfing gear from the previous chapter it's time to think about buying a board and gear. Faced with a showroom full of flashy looking boards, a mind-blowing array of gear and a hard-selling salesman the experience of buying your first equipment can be somewhat intimidating, particularly if, like most new surfers, you are on a very limited budget. It's important for your surfing and for your pocket that what you buy is right for you and that you are not wasting money on superfluous stuff.

The first move is to get rid of the pushy salesman! In other words, go to a reliable and honest dealer. One who will advise you just on what you need and who will work out the best deal in terms of price and requirements for your new adventure. Ask around experienced surfers and you will soon find out who are the rip-off merchants and who are the dealers with integrity.

Having found such a dealer, pour out your heart to him. Tell him how much money you have to spend on your new surf gear and ask his advice on what to buy at this stage so you can work up a budget. Don't forget the extras that may not be in the showroom, such as lessons, club fees and the like. Remember also that it is going to take you probably 12 months to learn to surf properly, so see what items you can purchase a little later (especially if you are on a budget) or if you can pay on a time basis.

Following are a few questions and answers to help you avoid the problems that come with buying surfing gear for the first time. Let's start with the board:

What size of board is best for a beginner?
The more width, length and thickness the board has the more stability it will have. So it follows that, within reason, a bigger board

The best dealers are those who specialise only in surfing gear.

Advice from a helpful dealer can save hassles in the early days of surfing.

will be easier for you in your early training sessions. A board with greater buoyancy and stability will enable you to concentrate on developing your skills without being frequently tipped off the board or having to constantly grab for the rails to keep your balance. But bear in mind that too long a board will be hard to turn and this will limit your ability to develop new techniques as you gain confidence and skills. So a medium-length board, or perhaps a mini-Mal, is probably the best for your first months. A full Mal can be rather limiting if you intend to graduate later to other types of surfing. A board about 8ft in length suits most beginner surfers.

Also well suited to beginners are 'soft-style' surfboards. These have a soft nose, rails and fins, which reduce the risk of injury to beginner surfers. All good surf schools use these boards.

What factors influence the size of a board?

The bigger you are the more buoyancy the board will need to support your weight. Buoyancy in the board comes with volume which, in turn, is dependent on thickness, length and width. There is no rule of thumb in terms of your height or weight because boards differ in volume according to design. You will need to discuss this with your dealer, but bear in mind that, at this stage in your surfing career, a medium to long board will always be better for learning than a very short board. It's not a bad idea to get yourself weighed and measured before going to see the dealer as he or she will then be better able to judge which type of board will suit you best.

How heavy or light?

Surfboards are made of a shaped foam blank encased in fibreglass, and fibreglass is measured in ounces per square yard (imperial measurement is still used). A boz cloth will give a strong and resilient board for most purposes, although as you get experienced you may prefer a lighter weight than the board you started with for better performance in small waves.

Where is the best place to buy a board?

Don't buy from newspaper advertisements and the like because you never know what you are buying. Be careful in buying a second-hand surfboard. As with second-hand cars, they can have hidden defects and the beautifully-coloured, sharp-looking board you bought from a display in a shop window may turn out to be a lemon. Also, avoid surf supermarkets or shops which carry a large range of surf goods; go for a specialist board dealer who has a wide range of new and second-hand boards and ask his advice. Since you are not only a customer at the time but a potential customer for the years ahead, if he is a wise operator he will give you good advice and maybe a good deal.

Second-hand or new?
Since the very first board will be used mainly just to get you going, this might not be the time to buy new. Once again, much depends on your friendly dealer. He may be able to cut you a better deal on a new board than a second-hand but, as a general rule, it is better to save your precious dollars until you have learned the basics and the direction your surfing is going. A second-hand board, chosen wisely, will usually save you money and suffice for your early training sessions. Then, when it's time to start thinking about comps, or when you have decided that a Mal or a short board, for example, is your scene, it is time to splurge on a new, perhaps even custom-built, board.

If I buy a second-hand surfboard with dings, can they be repaired?
Yes. As long as the board is basically sound, dings and scratches can be easily and satisfactorily repaired. Indeed, you will probably find your board already has dings if you bought it second-hand. Providing the ding has been repaired correctly it should not make much difference to the performance. Structural damage is a different matter altogether and you should not buy a board with any signs of serious damage.

What should I look out for when buying a second-hand board?
The main thing to look for is breaks or 'creases' (a board that has been bent across the width) because these can mean permanent structural damage. It's hard to repair a broken board without the repair being obvious (although if it has been totally spray-painted it might be somewhat suspect). Likewise, a crease is fairly easy to spot because it looks as though the board has been folded in one area. Make sure you examine all dings and blemishes

You need to be able to move comfortably at all times in your wetsuit.

carefully, especially if you are not buying from a reputable dealer, as there are unscrupulous people around and if you buy a bomb you won't enjoy your surfing.

Can I make a surfboard myself?

You can, but it won't really do much for your surfing. Surfboard design and construction is a highly skilled art and it is unlikely that you will be able to produce a board that responds like a professionally-built board. You will wind up feeling very frustrated because you won't get the most out of your surfing, even though you feel you have the skills. Let's face it, you can surf on Mum's ironing board if you want to, but you won't enjoy it!

From whom should I get advice: friend, expert or dealer?

Don't listen to friends: they might mean well but they also might not know what they are talking about. Speak with a recognised expert if you can find one. If you have built up a rapport with your dealer he will be the best source of assistance.

How many fins?

The number of fins fitted to your board is not all that important at this stage. Multi-fins are designed for speed in turns, but for training a single fin is fine. Generally speaking, the shape and number of fins is related to the increased performance of the board in certain conditions. You wouldn't fit the tyres used for Formula 1 racing cars on your family car, so don't worry about fitting fancy fins to your learning board. Multi- or single-fin is fine; other factors such as correct volume and stability are more important at this stage.

How many stringers?

Stringers are of no concern to a beginner providing the board is correctly built and has sufficient volume. When you become an expert and have your boards custom-built then is the time to talk to the shaper about stringers.

What shape tail?

For early surfing it's not all that important. A round tail is probably best—don't use a pintail—but take the advice of your dealer.

The right board and the right gear makes for relaxed, enjoyable surfing.

What shape nose?

The fuller the nose the more stable the board and the easier it is to paddle, but remember that a full nose can also create resistance to the water, so when paddling out it will be a little harder to get through the waves than with a fine, pointed nose. Once again, at the beginner stage stability is the main requirement, so a reasonably full nose is probably better than a very fine nose.

How much rocker?

Too much rocker pushes up the water so a moderate rocker is called for at this stage. Much depends on your weight and experience, so discuss this with your dealer when you're beginning to look for a board.

Should I buy grip or wax?

The choice is not too important but where you put it is, because it tells you where your feet should be when you are surfing. The experts prefer wax, at least on the deck, although many use grip near the tail. Modern grips are shaped to give better footing when pushing hard on the back foot and at this early stage, grip would probably be suitable both near the tail and in the middle of the board. If you decide to use wax, hard wax is best for warm weather, and soft for the winter days. Ask your dealer what brand he thinks is best for you.

Do I need a bag for the board?

Yes, especially if you travel on public transport. It's very easy to ding your board when clambering around on buses or trains. And if you're travelling by plane a bag is a must, with extra padding around the fins.

How do you pack a board for travel?

If you are travelling, particularly by air, you must pack your board thoroughly. Buy a specially padded travelling bag and proper fin guards, and stuff towels or padding all round the board when it is

The sea can be a tough place—this can happen even to the best of boards.

in its bag. And try to get it top-stowed in the aircraft hold so it doesn't get crushed. Most specially made bags have a sign on them requesting top stowage.

What size of leg rope?
The longer the better while you are learning. It will keep the board away from you when you wipeout, thus avoiding a fractured skull or similar injury. By the same token, as mentioned in the previous chapter, a long leggie can be dangerous when surfing near reefs or rocks as it can get snagged. Since you shouldn't be surfing over reefs or rocks as a beginner, the long leg rope will suit you best. As you get more used to the board and the surf you can change the length of the leg rope to suit.

Any specific type of wetsuit for a beginner?
It depends on the climate and season, and particularly the temperature of the air and water. A spring suit—short arms and legs—is the most versatile for temperate to warm climates, but you'll need a full steamer if it's cold. Read the previous chapter about wetsuits and then talk to your dealer before buying.

Should I buy a helmet?
It's a good move while you are a beginner since a nasty dump, even on sand, can give you a splitting headache or worse. As you become more experienced you may decide to leave the helmet at home when you are surfing the beach, but make sure you take it along when surfing near rocks or reefs. Some helmets have polaroid visors which help reduce the glare and UV rays from the sun. This is useful especially when you are spending a long time in the water.

Should I buy a rashie?
Definitely. Rashies are great for preventing chafe under a wet-suit—which is their main purpose—but they are also UV-proof, so you can wear one to avoid sun damage when the weather is

warm and you are not wearing a wetsuit. Be very aware of the sun; it is the surfer's greatest enemy and an insidious one at that—you don't realise the damage the sun is doing to your body until later in life when your surfing days are over.

How fragile is my new board?

You can damage a surfboard quite easily, so use commonsense and treat it with care. Don't drop it on the footpath or bang it around when loading it on the car. In the water most dings come from hitting another board or hitting something in the water. So handle it carefully, but remember that surfboards are not eggs!

Should I lay the board down fins up or deck up?

It doesn't really matter, as long as you put it down gently. But don't stand it on its rail—it can topple and become easily damaged.

WAVES

Three-quarters of the world's surface is covered with salt water, which is an awful lot of ocean, especially when you think that in some places it is almost 20 kilometres deep. There is no risk that surfers will ever run out of waves because that water is constantly moving and it moves in different areas—which is why there are waves that create good surf one day and poor surfing conditions the next.

Waves are caused by wind blowing across the surface of the sea. The wind may not be in the immediate vicinity, because local winds build up only small surface waves; most good surf is the result of storms way out at sea.

Imagine throwing a small rock into a pool: the ripples from the splash radiate outwards to the edge of the pool. That, effectively, is what happens when a big storm blows up in the ocean. The storm, like the rock, creates a disturbance in the water which sends swells radiating outwards across the ocean. These swells can travel long distances and they reach the coastline in the form of big waves, which break on the headlands and beaches, creating top surfing conditions to the delight of the surfer.

Such waves can travel many thousands of kilometres from the storm centre to the nearest coastline and it's not uncommon for waves from the same storm to cause big waves on both sides of an ocean—the coasts of Australia and New Zealand, for example, or Hawaii and California. Of course it would have to be a big storm to cover such vast tracts of ocean, such as a cyclone or a hurricane.

However, the waves travelling across the oceans are not the prime concern of surfers—it's what happens to those waves when they reach the coast. Out at sea they are all much the same: symmetrical and fairly even and they roll along consistently with a circular action below the surface. But when they move into the shallow water of the coastal areas they change shape due to the effect of the coastal geography and the changing format of the sea bed. It is this shape that determines whether they are good surf waves or not, and it is the different coastal features and the shape of the sea bed that create top surfing conditions at some beaches and ordinary waves at another.

Types of waves

There are basically two types of waves of interest to surfers: wind waves and swell waves. While they are both created the same way—by wind blowing across the surface of the water—they are totally different in character. Wind waves are the short, choppy waves that are mostly broken, rarely very big and build up on blustery, windy days. While they are sometimes surfable, mostly as 'shoreys' (inshore waves) close to the beach, they usually provide pretty ordinary conditions for board-riding.

Swell waves, on the other hand, are what surfers look for. These are the waves, described earlier, that are created by storms out at sea and which have rolled across the oceans, gaining size and power, until they rear up as they get into shallow water sometimes to heights of 7 metres and more. These are the waves that produce sheer walls, magnificent barrels and extensive right- and left-handers which so delight the serious surfer's heart!

Formation of a wave

In deep water a wave rolls along with a fairly symmetrical circular action, but as it moves in towards the shallow water of the coast, it begins to 'feel bottom'. The lower part of the wave is dragged back by the friction of the sea bed while the top of the wave continues on with the momentum built up in its travel across the ocean. As the wave approaches the beach where the water gets even shallower, the drag of the bottom holds back the lower part of the wave even more until the top part, still pushing forward, literally trips over itself. The bottom of the wave stops and the top continues forward, causing the water to rear up and fall forward in the typical surf wave configuration. As a general rule, a wave breaks when the depth of water is around 1.3 times the height of the wave.

Just what shape the wave takes before it breaks depends mainly on the nature of the sea bottom and this explains why some beaches or headlands, where sandbanks or reefs under the water create excellent surf waves whenever good ocean swells roll in, are recognised as being top surfing spots. Waimea Bay in Hawaii, G-land in Indonesia and Margaret River in Australia are areas typical of such spots.

Of course the topography of the sea bed does not always remain constant. Sandbanks move, rips scour out channels and tides cause the depth of water to change and, as a result, the character of the waves is affected. For this reason it is always important to study the waves carefully before making any attempt to paddle out, no matter where you are planning to surf or what the previous conditions were like. Where there were perfect surfing conditions the last time you visited, the waves could soon be very ordinary. Where the waves were lousy six hours ago at low tide, they may be cranking as the tide reaches its peak.

After crossing the ocean, a big swell creates excellent surf.

The form of the sea bed is the main factor in the waves' shape.

A shallow beach has waves that break well out from the shore and roll in as 'foamies'.

Beach break

There are several factors that affect the shape of beach waves, the most prominent being the nature of the sea bed immediately off the beach. A steep beach, where the sea bed drops away quickly and where deep water almost reaches sand, is likely to create steep, short waves that start to build close to the shore and break fairly quickly. By contrast, a shallow beach, where the depth of water hardly changes for some distance out, is more likely to provide good surfing waves that form well offshore and roll in for some considerable distance, cresting and breaking gradually along their length.

In a sea bed with a channel the waves take up a deep-water appearance, rolling in closer to shore before breaking, whereas shallow sandbanks off the beach will cause the waves to break as they cross the bank, dissolving into a mess of white water that offers nothing to the surfer. This is a typical beach wave pattern and often it is where the channel runs between sandbanks that some of the best surfing conditions can be found. However, that is a very basic premise as there are other factors which affect the shape of the wave. Again, it is important to spend time on the beach studying the waves before paddling out.

Point break

If you have ever wondered why waves almost always break parallel to a beach, think again about the drag of the sea bed on the bottom of the wave which causes it to break. If a wave approaches the shore at an angle, the inshore end of the wave moves first into shallow water and the drag of the sea bed at that end of the wave causes it to slow and pull the rest of the wave round, rather like a wheeling line of soldiers, so that it breaks evenly along the beach.

Much the same conditions create a point break. As a wave moving along a coastline strikes a point or headland, its progress

Waves around a headland or its offshore reefs create good point break conditions.

at that end is impeded by the drag of the headland and the rest of the wave 'wheels' round the point. The water is usually shallower at the shore end of the wave, so it begins to break there, and the break gradually moves along the wave as it wheels round into the shallower water. A good point break can provide some of the finest surfing waves.

Reef break

The shape and depth of an offshore reef has a direct influence on the shape of a wave rolling over it. The swells rolling in from the sea can rear up steeply as the wave trips over its feet and dumps on a shallow reef. Depending on the underwater shape of the reef and the angle at which the wave strikes, it may form good surf waves with the potential for good barrels. This type of situation is often found on coral reefs since coral grows only in relatively shallow water, impeding the waves coming in from deep water. Needless to say, this also creates extremely dangerous surfing conditions, since being dumped at any time can risk injury, but being dumped on coral can be life-threatening. Less hazardous, but also less exciting to ride are the fat waves created on deep reefs—the infamous 'bomboras' found in Australia. These waves build to a considerable height but do not usually form such steep walls.

The effects of wind on waves

Apart from creating the waves in the first place, wind can have a strong influence on the shape of the wave as it breaks along the shoreline. Generally speaking, an onshore wind does not create very favourable surfing conditions. It pushes the top of the wave forward, causing it to break too soon and the result is mushy, broken surf which few surfers enjoy.

By contrast, a wind blowing off the shore tends to hold up the wave as it starts to break, causing it to become hollow and develop a strong wall which often breaks in a perfect barrel shape. Even if it doesn't create a tube an offshore wind will usually provide good surfing conditions. In warm climates these conditions can be experienced almost every day, caused by what is known as the 'land breeze' and 'sea breeze' phenomena.

Land and sea breezes

When the sun heats up the land during the day it sets off rising thermal air currents which create a vacuum over the hot land mass. This vacuum drags in cool air from the sea, creating an onshore breeze, which usually starts during the morning and increases during the afternoon as the land gets hotter. This is known as the sea breeze.

At night the land cools down so the process is reversed: warm air rises off the sea creating a vacuum into which cool air from the now-cold land flows. This is the offshore or land breeze which builds up through the night and is at its maximum around dawn. Hence some of the best-shaped waves are found early in the morning when the land breeze holds up the oncoming waves and creates fine surfing conditions. Every surfer has, at some stage, enjoyed the benefits of the 'early'—an early morning surf with the offshore wind producing ideal conditions.

Tides and waves

Tides ebb and flow twice a day, creating two high tides and two lows tides within each 24 hours—and one hour later each day. Tides are caused mainly by the phases of the moon, but we won't go into such details in this book. However, it is important to understand the effect tides have on waves and thus on surfing conditions. Tides are consistent and predictable, so much so that the times and heights of each tide are provided in annual tide tables. It is possible to anticipate changes in surfing conditions by knowing the tidal movements—when they are likely to occur at a specific beach or point and what they will do to the surf.

Early morning land breezes blowing off the beach create the best conditions for surfing.

The main effect tides have on surfing conditions is to the depth of the water over banks and reefs and thus the shape of the waves at those spots. A totally different wave can be expected over a reef at high tide, for example, when it has perhaps 3 metres of water over it than at low tide when it has only 1 metre. And while 2-metre tides are fairly commonplace in many parts of the world, there are places where the tide can rise and fall 10 metres or more! Imagine what that could do to the shape of a wave!

If you are free surfing, knowing the tidal movements may not be all that important, but for competition surfing it is vital to know how the waves are changing through the duration of the competition as a result of tide movements. Tide tables and tidal predictions are given in newspapers and other media, so keeping an eye on the tide shouldn't be too difficult.

Sets

Apart from the fact that there are big waves on stormy days and on quiet days it's best to put away the board and get out the fishing rods, waves vary in size all the time. When all outside influences are steady and the waves are fairly consistent there will still be different wave sizes and shapes coming through. Larger than average groups or 'sets' of waves roll in at fairly regular intervals. These can be seen approaching and usually provide excellent opportunities to pick up points in a contest or to catch a good wave if you are just free surfing.

A set of big waves is sometimes formed by waves from two different sources merging. They might originate from two separate storms out at sea, or one set of waves might have been reflected from a land mass. Even the topography of the sea bed can cause waves to move in different directions which, when they combine, create a bigger than average set as they move into the beach. Whatever the cause, the smart surfer will keep his or his eye on the horizon and watch for the approach of a good set, then position him or herself to take advantage of them.

Sets are easily visible as they approach the shore.

WAVE TALK

Although they vary around the world, most terms used to describe waves are universal. Following are the main ones:

Wave height: the height of the wave, measured in various ways in different surfing zones.

Crest: the top of the wave.

Trough: the depression between two waves.

Face: the front of the wave.

Back: the rear or back slope of the wave.

Wall: the steep, sheer face of a rearing wave.

Barrel: a tunnel or hollow under the crest of a wave as it rolls over.

Tube: another name for the barrel.

Fat wave: a thick, sloping wave with no wall and often a broken crest.

Hollow wave: a wave about to break with a concave face.

Closed out: a wave which breaks evenly along its entire length.

Left-hander: wave where the break is on the right of the surfer.

Right-hander: wave where the break is on the left of the surfer.

Pocket: the point at which the break is at the top of the wave.

Ordinary: poor surf.

Messy: broken surf.

Cranking: good surf running.

Lip: the top edge of the wave.

Shoulder: the unbroken part of the wave next to the break.

Sucking: the bottom of the wave drawing back.

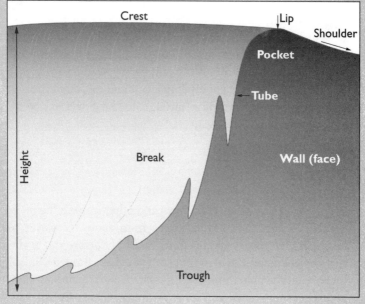

Parts of a wave

PREPARING TO SURF

As with any sport, preparation is the key factor to success in surfing. It is important whether you are just going out for a pleasant afternoon surf with a couple of mates or whether you are entering a tough surf contest. Of course, if you are taking part in a contest preparation is doubly important and can often mean the difference between winning through to the finals and getting knocked out in the first heat.

UV rays

Forget sharks, jellyfish, coral reefs and other nasties; the biggest menace to a surfer's health comes from above the waves, not below. It's not always an easy thing to do, but before you begin to surf anywhere think of skin cancer. If you don't want to think of it in those terms, then think of it this way: How long do you want to go on surfing? Until you are 25? Thirty? Thirty-five, if you're lucky? That bright, warm sunshine which gives you such a good feeling today may be shortening your life so that in the years ahead, while your mates are still surfing, you will be watching them from a wheelchair, nursing the one leg they haven't yet cut off. And that's if you're lucky—a lot of young guys who had years and years of surfing ahead of them are now lying in the graveyard because they didn't take care in the sun.

Don't get the idea that it is just the direct rays of the sun that cause the damage—reflection from the sea, surf and the beach can be damaging both to the skin and the eyes. Even overcast days are not safe; indeed, they can be deceptively dangerous and the effect of the damaging UV rays can be worse than on a sunny day. You might get away with board shorts and sun cream in the very early morning before the sun's strength builds up, but even then it's a wise move to keep your top half covered with a T-shirt or rashie. If you'd rather be surfing than lying in hospital, take care to keep out those nasty UV rays.

If you don't care and are going to take a chance, then at least cover the exposed parts of your body with a water-resistant SPF15—or greater—sun cream or zinc. Take particular care with your face; your nose and ears are very vulnerable and you won't grab too much attention from the opposite sex on the beach if your nose or one ear has been removed by surgery! If you are wearing a steamer you should be fairly well covered—just use cream on your face, hands and feet—but if you are wearing a spring suit, singlet or some other cut-down wetsuit, then make sure your exposed skin is covered with zinc or SPF cream.

Wetsuits

It is important that your wetsuit fits closely, especially when you are surfing in cold water. It's not the material of the wetsuit that insulates your body against the cold, it's the layer of water trapped between the suit and your body. Water is a poor conductor of heat and therefore the water trapped against your body prevents your

A sensible outfit for surfing in sunny weather: board shorts and rashie.

body heat from escaping. The wetsuit is merely a means of holding that layer of water in place against your body. So a loose-fitting wetsuit allows the water to move around and escape, taking your body heat with it. Then a new layer of water comes into the wetsuit to replace it and that's usually very cold!

The rashie goes on first, inside out to the normal way of wearing clothes in order to prevent chafe from the wetsuit. Your swimmers should be sufficient to prevent chafe on the lower regions of your body. If the wetsuit is too tight to pull on, fit a plastic bag over your arms or legs and you will find the wetsuit will slip on quite easily. Take the plastic bag off afterwards, of course!

If you find you are having trouble zipping up the back of the wetsuit get someone to do it for you, because an incorrectly zipped back seam can let in water and defeat the purpose of the wetsuit. Make sure the flaps are correctly laid over before the zipper is

A plastic bag enables even the tightest wetsuit to slip on easily.

Many top surfers prefer to wax their boards where the front foot is positioned.

secured and ensure that the fit of the collar is nice and tight or, once again, you will get annoying—and chilly—leaks that spoil the enjoyment of your surf.

Preparing the board

With the board out of its bag it's time to get it ready for your first run. Take a quick check to see it has not suffered any damage in transit, especially if you have been travelling by air, which is a notorious way to wreck a surfboard (see Chapter Two), and if need be clean off the old wax with a comb or scraper and stash it in a waste bin. (Don't leave it lying around—that's littering.) Either use new wax or, if there is plenty left, comb it in a cross pattern to provide better grip. If your board has grip, check it out to see that it is clean and is not coming unstuck anywhere. There is nothing worse than getting up on a wave only to have the grip slip off the moment you put pressure on it.

Wax or grip?

Wax comes in a wide variety of types and qualities. Generally, you should use hard wax in warm temperatures and softer wax in cold temperatures, but there are other factors involved and you will need advice on this one. Start waxing around the middle of the board where your front foot will be placed (if you don't already have grip there, of course). Rub the wax on firmly until it provides a fair amount of friction, then repeat the exercise near the tail of the board where your back foot will be located. Many good surfers fit grip to the tail and use wax in the middle of the board. Others use grip in both places, while some prefer no grip at all and rely solely on wax. The choice is a personal one and with experience you will find which suits you best. However, for beginners grip is probably the easiest and most suitable.

One end of the leg rope is secured to the board's tail and the other end to your back leg.

Leg ropes

Leg ropes are fitted to a socket located near the tail of the board. The usual fitting has a pin located in this socket and generally a light piece of synthetic cord in the form of a loop is passed around this pin. This cord can be left in place when you change leg ropes so that the new leggie can be quickly attached to it rather than having to thread a new cord each time. A velcro strap on the inside end of the leggie is looped through the cord and this secures the rope to the board. A velcro strap at the other end of the leggie secures it to your ankle. Which leg should the leggie be attached to? Why, the back leg, of course!

Loosening up

You've got your wetsuit on, the board is ready and the surf's cranking. But there is still more to do before you plunge in. The next step is one taken by every serious surfer, and one that is essential if you are to gain the full benefit and enjoyment from your surfing. Ten minutes of stretching exercises on the beach will loosen up jaded, unused muscles and not only make your surfing more relaxed and enjoyable, but will prevent nasty stress injuries which can put an end to your surfing for the next few days.

Stretching exercises are an integral part of serious surfing. Watch the pros at competitions; you will see them go through a solid routine of exercises before getting in the water. Even amateur surfers do it because they know how painful and frustrating stress injuries can be. Novices will benefit as much as pros because if you haven't done much surfing before, your muscles are not ready for the stresses they are going to encounter. Watching the pros or talking to a sports physio will indicate the sort of stretches you should be doing. Get advice from any surf club or athletics organisation, or develop your own system, providing it stretches the muscles you are likely to use while surfing.

Stretching is vitally important before surfing if you want to avoid muscle injury.

Watching the waves

Now that you have completed all your preparations, you can't wait
to get out in the water. But if you just run down the beach, throw
your board into the white water and head out for the first wave,
you are quite likely to find yourself back on the beach in seconds,
head over turkey, wondering what steamroller just ran over you!
Either that or an hour later, totally exhausted, you will still be try-
ing to get out through waves which seem hell-bent on pushing
you back towards the beach, however furiously you paddle. This
whole endeavour can be particularly frustrating when you notice
that the surfers who jumped into the water at the same time as
you are now catching their fifth or sixth wave, while you haven't
even got out to the break!

This is the sort of problem you will encounter if you don't sit down on the beach and study the surf before rushing in. Like your stretching exercises, a few minutes spent sitting on the beach can pay great dividends when you get into the water. Apart from the question of getting out easily, studying the surf can indicate where the best waves are and where you should paddle out in order to catch the sort of waves that will suit you best.

Paddling out

Paddling out can be a nightmare for some beginner surfers, so it's not a bad idea to get into the paddling technique in still water before fronting up to those big waves. Develop and improve your techniques in the quiet water of a swimming pool or a river, so that when you throw your board into the surf you will have the confidence as well as the technique to paddle out through the white water with relative ease.

Rips

In Chapter Three we talked about the sandbanks and channels that make up the structure of a beach. Obviously, you wouldn't try to power out through the white water on a bank since, apart from getting pounded to pieces, you will be using up unnecessary energy getting nowhere. A channel has less white water, which means the waves will be easier to push through and your passage out will be less exhausting. More importantly, there is a chance that the channel will have a rip.

Rips, which are so dangerous for swimmers, help surfers get out through the break quickly and easily. With practice you will soon know how to identify the rips, but if in doubt, just watch where experienced surfers go out and follow them. Rips are caused by the backwash of waves funnelling out to sea from the beach, usually through a scoured channel. If the waves break parallel to the beach the rips can be encountered at regular points along it, but if the waves are angled to the beach then the strongest rips will be found in the corners. But since the rips on each beach are different and often vary from day to day, it is important to take time out to study the waves before you begin surfing—they will tell you where the rips are located.

Where to surf

Another reason for studying the waves is to determine just where is the best surf. Obviously if you are a first-timer, you need to feel your way with the smaller inshore waves, but as you progress you will be keen to get out the back and pick up some bigger waves.

Studying the waves before plunging in will save a lot of frustration and unnecessary effort.

The way in which waves break indicate the location of rips, banks and good surfing spots.

This is also a good time to watch the sets and see how frequently they move in and the quality of waves they offer. Indeed, it is a time to take an overall view of what you can expect when you get out there. As you gain experience you can make a fairly accurate assessment of the surfing conditions you will encounter. If one area is constantly closing out, for example, you would need to avoid that. You might then spot an area with a choice of right- or left-handers. White water indicating a sandbank is an area to avoid, since being dumped on a shallow bank can be a board-busting experience.

THE FIRST SURF

With all the preparation done, it's time for the real action to start. Enough of the beach, now into the water.

Paddling out

After watching the surf from the beach, you will know the best spot to paddle out, so with your leg rope secured around your back ankle you can move into the water. Depending on the surf and the nature of the beach you may be able to walk out some distance, or you may have to start paddling right from the beach. Pick your moment, then launch your board over a wave, at the same time falling onto it and beginning to paddle. Your chest should be positioned about one-third of the way back from the nose and your arms should be free to stroke down each side of the board. If you have a long board your feet may come up onto the deck so that you are lying along the full length and just paddling with your

Paddling out can be frightening for beginners!

arms. On a short board, especially if you are tall, your feet may be hanging over the tail.

If you are paddling out in a rip and suddenly find yourself heading out to sea at speed, don't panic. A rip is not such a problem for surfers as it can be for swimmers because you have your board for support. If swimmers took a page out of a surfer's book and let the rip take them, instead of fighting it to the point of exhaustion, there would be far fewer fatalities on our beaches.

So relax and let the rip take you out until the strength of the flow eases and you can paddle comfortably across and out of it. It shouldn't be long before you find your spot and are in a good position to catch a wave.

Duck diving

As you paddle out you will have to fight your way through the oncoming waves. First out from the beach will be the broken white water and then the shories or smaller waves; these shouldn't create much of a problem. But once you get farther out you will start to hit the big breaking waves which can sometimes be hard to get through. Between the waves you can make good progress, but when they rear up and break they can hit hard. With the passing of each wave you will find yourself halfway back to the beach, having lost all the ground you made between them. This can be exhausting as well as frustrating so you need to develop techniques to easily get through these breaking waves.

There are a number of methods of doing this. Some involve rolling the board somewhat in the style of a canoeist's 'Eskimo roll'—best with long boards. Some surfers prefer to abandon the board on the end of the leg rope while they dive under the wave, collecting the board again when the wave passes. But the most widely used system is the duck dive in which both the surfer and board dive together under the wave and bob up again when the wave has passed. This enables you to get under the worst of the breaking water and avoid being swept back while staying on your board. Timing is the key factor in this, because if you time your dive correctly the wave will slide over you; if you miscalculate you will find the wave will carry you back to the beach. The procedure for a duck dive is as follows:

1 As the oncoming wave moves down on you, quickly draw your knees up so that you are effectively in a kneeling position on the board.
2 Just before the wave strikes, push the nose down hard and at the same time lower your head and shoulders so that you literally duck under the wave.
3 As the wave passes over you, push the board down with your knees so that your body passes under the breaking wave and pull the nose up.
4 If you have handled the manoeuvre correctly you should bob up behind the wave without having gone backwards too far. Start paddling again and repeat the manoeuvre with each wave until you are through the break.

A good wave and a good spot for take-off.

The right spot

You will already have some idea of where you intend to start surfing by watching the waves from the beach. But things look a whole
lot different when you are out in the water and you now have to
take it a step further and find out just where the right spot is for
take-off. It will take a while but once you have found a good spot
and have caught a couple of waves look for a reference point on
shore so that you can come back to it time and again. This can be
anything that doesn't move: a tree, a house, a sand dune or whatever. Each time you paddle back to your spot aim to line up with
the same reference point and, although that may not give you the
best waves every time, if you picked it right the first time it will at
least put you in a position where you know you can catch a wave.
The more waves you catch, the more you will get to know the right
spot and adjust your original reference point so that each time you
paddle back you can quickly get into position for the next wave. In

a contest this can be a very useful technique as it will get you into position for the maximum number of waves during your heat.

Picking the right wave

It makes good sense, if you are a beginner, to work the shories first and then when you feel confident get out the back among the big waves. It takes a while to get used to your board and you will not be concentrating too much on what you are doing if you are in a flat panic suddenly screaming down the face of a 2-metre wave with your legs going in all the wrong directions.

So when watching the waves from the beach, forget what's going on out the back and watch the shories. Select a spot where you can try out both your board and yourself without too much risk of damage to either or to other people; a spot where the waves are big enough to give you a nice ride but won't overpower you or your board. At this stage, don't worry too much about the waves' shape—although clean, unbroken waves will give you a nicer ride— even small, ordinary waves are all you need right now so you can get the feel of what happens when your board starts moving.

Don't rush to get up. Tummy surfing will teach you a lot about the way the board reacts.

Paddle out to a suitable spot and position yourself to watch the oncoming waves. Look for one that is big enough to get you going. Watch it approach and, if possible, paddle around to get yourself into a position where it will strike you just before it breaks. As the wave reaches you line up the board so it is facing shorewards and wait for the lift at the back of the board that will tell you the wave has arrived. Immediately paddle furiously. Try to pick up the momentum of the wave so you stay with it and don't let it pass under you. If you're lucky or if you have done all the right things, suddenly you will feel the board surge forward. If you are unlucky it will fall back sluggishly and let the wave pass under. Oh well, next one!

Tummy surfing first!

When you feel the board surge forward to catch the wave, stop paddling and grab the rails. At this stage don't attempt to get up; it's best to get the feel of the board while you have things under control. Getting up comes later. By shifting your weight and turning the board by the rails you will find you can manoeuvre the board across the face of the wave, so spend some time getting the feel of this and learning how your board reacts.

Getting the feel of your board is something you can only do with repeated practice and to start by lying down is a good way initially because you can concentrate solely on this and not worry about things like standing up and balance. In particular, note how the board reacts to movements of your body. Deliberately shift your weight from side to side or backwards and forwards to understand what happens when you do this. Turn the board by the rails as you run down the face of the waves and note the effect. The knowledge you gain from these basic actions will help you when you start real surfing. Don't worry if the more experienced surfers rubbish you for doing it on your tummy; that's how most of them started—although, of course, they would never admit it.

The moment of truth—take-off!

Taking off

The secret of getting a good start depends on two things: timing the take-off and picking the right spot on the wave. Of the two, timing is probably the most important because if you pick the wrong place on the wave you might still have a chance to recover and get some sort of surf out of it, but if you miss the timing you will lose the wave altogether.

As a wave approaches, before you give it a try you have to determine if you are in the right position. Study the wave and try to anticipate where it will start to break. You should know if it's going to be a left- or right-hander and start to move so that you can position yourself on the shoulder just clear of the break. This is the ideal spot in which to take off. If you are too close to the break you will be dumped or lose it in the broken water; if you are too far away there will not be sufficient momentum in the shoulder to get you going. Ideally, you want to make your run close to the break and moving away from it, but not so far that there is insufficient power in the wave.

Paddle quickly across the oncoming wave as it approaches, then swing the board round and line up with the wave. At this point you should be right under the face so that as the wave lifts the board, you are close to the break and ready to go. As you feel it lift and start to push you forward, paddle furiously. This is the moment of truth: if you've done everything right you will suddenly feel that surge of exhilaration as the board gets up and starts flying. Turn it across the wave away from the break and start surfing!

If the board is not moving fast enough or the wave is not pushing it ahead sufficiently, then you have a choice: keep on paddling and hope to pick up enough momentum to keep going, or drop back and wait for the next wave. Like every other aspect of surfing, you will need a lot of practice before you get it right.

Standing up

So far you have been doing all this on your tummy. Now that you have your timing right and you've got the feel of the board it's time to take the big step—standing up! Because you have been learning all the basics while lying on your tummy, you will be able to catch the wave without having to think too much about that part of it—you can now concentrate solely on getting to your feet. So let's take it from the moment the board surges forward and you know you have caught the wave. This is the big one, the moment when it all comes together. Some instructors favour a step-by-step approach such as kneeling first, but it's probably best to take one giant step and go from tummy to feet in almost a single movement. Almost, because in fact it is really two movements, as you will see, though once you become proficient at it, it will seem like one movement.

Pick the right waves to begin with. If you try to stand up in 2-metre waves you will become disheartened and may even damage yourself or your board. Pick a relatively quiet day with low surf to start with and build up as you gain skills and confidence. It will take a lot of practice because not only do you have to get to your feet, but you have to maintain your balance and also keep the board under control—and that's a big ask! The secret is start small and build up. The routine for standing up can vary from surfer to surfer, but the basic pattern will be as follows:

1 As the board starts to move down the wave, stop paddling and with both hands grip the rails underneath your shoulders.
2 When you are in this position jump your feet up onto the board while still holding the rails. Don't do it in easy stages such as kneeling then climbing to your feet; make sure you jump straight to your feet in one movement while still bent over holding the rails.
3 From the bent position, release the rails and stand up straight. Spread your feet wide—wider than your shoulders—with your legs bent at around 90 degrees.
4 Immediately get into a balanced position with your feet wide, legs bent and back straight. Look ahead over the nose of the board and spread your arms out to help you balance.
5 Start off going straight ahead, then move onto unbroken waves and start turning the board across the face. From here on it is all practice.

It sounds easy, but in fact it is one of the hardest of all surfing techniques to learn because it is the basis of all surfing and a big step in your training; unless you can stand on the board you can't surf. It will take a while to get the hang of it and you will go through weeks, perhaps months, of frustration before it falls into place, but keep in mind through that period that once you have mastered this step you are really into surfing and that, after all, is what it's all about.

A fine action shot showing good stance and balance.

Jump onto your feet, with knees bent and arms outstretched to balance, and you are standing!

DEVELOPING THE SKILLS

From the time you first stand up on your board the world of surfing comes within your reach. Now you can choose the type of surfing you want to do and start to develop your skills. You may favour the long boards or mini-Mals, or you might prefer the snappy short boards—much depends on your age, your physical ability and what you want to get out of surfing. Older surfers can forget the tiny short boards that youngsters flip so exuberantly off the tops of the waves—that takes enormous physical effort. The stately Mals or mini-Mals will provide just as much fun and can be as competitive as the smaller boards. The middle range will suit most beginner surfers since these boards are big enough to provide a considerable amount of stability yet small enough to throw around on the face of a wave. On the other hand, if you are young, very fit and adventurous, short boards provide the ultimate test of stamina and skill in the surf.

If you fit the fit and adventurous description, your aim will probably be to make it into high-profile competition. This is the cutting edge of surfing, where your skills are challenged by the

Top action. A technique like this requires a lot of practice.

best in the game and your ability and dedication are stretched to breaking point. But like all sporting challenges, arriving at this stage takes years of hard work and dedication and, although it is mentioned briefly in this book by way of giving newcomers a taste of what they can achieve in surfing, it is not really a subject of discussion for beginners.

Whatever your choice of board or surfing style, the first step in achieving success is practice; lots and lots of practice. You can't spend too much time in the surf if your aim is to become a proficient surfer. Like other sports that depend on the elements, every day in surfing is a new experience. So you don't just learn the basics and then think you have got it beaten, you have to take up the new challenges the waves offer every day and through every sea condition.

But enough of the dreaming—back to the wave which you have just mastered by standing up on your board and riding it right into the beach. That's step one. Now to develop the techniques which will move you up the ladder towards being a proficient and competent surfer. For the most part, these skills are learned with practice—of which you can't get too much—and mostly on short and medium-length boards. Long boards and Mals may adopt some of the turns, but it goes without saying that the longer boards are not as manoeuvrable as the short, snappy boards when it comes to the more advanced techniques.

Bottom turn

Once you have mastered the art of catching the wave, standing up and making a run down the face of the wave you need to learn how to turn the board at the bottom. Your arms are an important tool in this manoeuvre, as with most surfing techniques, for they help with your balance and good balance is an essential part of surfing. Put simply, your leading arm should be stretched out or 'pointing' in the direction you are aiming to go while your other arm moves around as required to help keep your balance. As with sports such as skiing and skating, you will learn with practice how important your arms are and how you must use them to not only maintain your balance but also to improve your performance, especially in tight manoeuvres.

Your feet, in the meantime, should be strategically placed to control the board with your legs bent ('compressed'). You can surf with either foot forward, whichever feels best for you. If you surf with your left foot forward you are known as a 'natural'; with your right foot forward you are said to be 'goofy footed'. Moving your feet towards the rear of the board tends to provide more versatility in manoeuvring; moving them too far forward is likely to

Setting up for a bottom turn. Note where the surfer is looking.

Into the bottom and turn, ready to run back up the face.

nose-dive the board. So for a bottom turn you should have your front foot somewhere around the middle of the board and your back foot near the tail where the grip or wax will give good control every time you turn.

As you sweep down to the bottom of the face, you will be looking to perform a bottom turn to climb back up the wave. The following procedure indicates the basic steps for this:

1   Look up towards the top of the wave in the direction you intend to turn and bend ('compress') your legs.
2   Move your front arm and upper body in the direction you intend to turn.
3   Straighten ('extend') your legs while leaning into the wave and rotate the board.
4   As the board sweeps up through the turn compress your legs again, ready for the run up the face and the next manoeuvre—the top turn.

Top turn

Maximum speed and power in a wave is located near the pocket—the area close to the lip where the wave begins to break. However, as a beginner, it's not a wise procedure to attempt any of the turns too close to the lip unless the waves are relatively small. Keep the bottom and top turns well within the face of the wave, especially big waves. Spend time perfecting these because they are the basic manoeuvres that later will enable you to build up to the spectacular turns the pros use to demonstrate their skills.

A top turn involves a similar technique to the bottom turn, but is carried out at the top of the wave. The procedure is as follows:

1   As the board moves up towards the top of the wave compress your legs and look down.
2   When close to the top look in the direction you intend to turn.

A perfect top turn.

3 Extend your legs and rotate the board, turning your front arm
   and body round as the board sweeps into the turn.
4 As you complete the turn and head back down the wave pick up
   your normal surfing stance.

Esses

With the basic top and bottom turns mastered you need to now
become totally confident with them so you can perform them
almost instinctively. This will enable you to think about extending
to more advanced manoeuvres. A good exercise to familiarise
yourself with these is to combine them in a series of what are
sometimes called 'esses'. You sweep your board across the face of
the wave in wide, sweeping turns, running up into a top turn, then

'Esses' are good practice for mastering top and bottom turns.

across and down the wave into a bottom turn. Repeating this manoeuvre develops your control over the board, firstly in small waves, then in bigger and bigger waves, until you gain total confidence in handling your board through most conditions.

Esses are not only good training for most surfing skills, they also make for very pleasant and relaxed surfing. Some people are content just to enjoy riding the waves in this way, but most like to develop them into more challenging manoeuvres such as cut-backs or re-entries. Practising the basic turns will provide incentive to develop those skills, for it is a relatively small step from a sharp top turn to a snapback or reo.

Teaching the more advanced skills is not really practicable in a book; you learn those out on the water where your personal approach and talent come to bear. But the basics of some of the better known manoeuvres are described here to give you a foundation on which to base your own techniques.

Cut-back

This is a development of a top turn and is made at the top of the wave, usually well out on the shoulder and away from the pocket. It is aimed at getting you back into the power area of the wave. The basic steps are as follows:

1   You are heading across the face of the wave.
2   When you feel the wave start to lose power, head back up to the top using the bottom turn technique.
3   At the top, make a hard top turn.
4   Continue this turn down the face of the wave until you are heading back into the break.
5   Sweep up onto the lip and, as you hit it, rotate the board, using the broken water to help swing the board round, and head it back down the face of the wave.
6   You have completed a cut-back. Pick up surfing as before.

Cut-back.

Re-entry.

Re-entry (reo)

1 Complete a normal bottom turn but make it as deep and hard as possible.
2 When climbing up the face gain as much speed as you can and aim for the lip.
3 Prepare for a radical turn at the top.
4 When the board hits the lip, rotate your arms.
5 Push the tail round with your back foot using your front foot to aim the board back into the break.
6 Turn the board hard back, pivoting it with your hips.
7 Allow your head and shoulders to follow until you resume the normal surfing stance as the board heads back down and across the face of the wave.

Floater

A favourite with most surfers, this exciting manoeuvre will develop as you master your top turns. It involves getting the board up on the lip, floating across the top of the wave and coming back down with the lip. It is an exercise in timing and balance and requires great control. The basic steps are as follows:

1 From the bottom of the wave turn and race up the face towards the lip with speed.
2 At the lip, start a top turn, but instead of completing it straighten the board and float across the lip just in front of the break. This involves centring your weight across the board while maintaining forward movement.
3 As the wave breaks under you drop down the face, bringing the board under control once again.
4 Pick up surfing as normal.

Floater.

Snap-back.

Air.

Snap-back

A spectacular manoeuvre that always catches the eye because it throws a fan of spray up behind the board as the surfer sweeps through the turn at the top of the wave. You need to find power pockets to produce the best snap turns.

1 Pick up speed across or down the wave, look up and select your spot at the top.
2 Make a hard bottom turn and race up the wave towards the lip. Bend your legs and transfer your weight to the inside rail.
3 At the lip, extend your legs for maximum power then rotate your upper body hard in the direction of the break, pushing the board round with your extended legs.
4 As the board snaps round on the rail, centre your weight again and concentrate on bringing the board under control as it drops back down the face.

Air

Flying off the lip into space is not only a spectacular manoeuvre to watch, it is a big adrenaline rush for the surfer.

1 As with a snap-back, look up as you race across the face of a wave and select a launching point.
2 Pick up a lot of speed and race up to the section of the lip you have selected, keeping your speed up as much as possible.
3 As you hit the lip launch the board off it, compressing your legs, and rotate to bring the board back to the wave.
4 Keep your weight centred over the board as much as possible so you have control when you land.
5 Pick up your surfing as you come back down the wave.

The barrel, or tube.

Barrels (tubes)

Nothing is more eye-catching than a surfer riding through a barrel and 'spitting' out the end—and nothing is more exhilarating for the board-rider. It's a manoeuvre that requires not only a lot of skill, but a great deal of luck with the wave. In places like the infamous Pipeline of Hawaii the waves are more reliable in shape and good barrels more frequent, but wherever you attempt to ride a barrel you will need to study the waves well beforehand.

1 Position yourself where you expect the lip to curl and take off just ahead of the break.
2 Race steeply down the face of the wave, just keeping ahead of the break, then level out with your board and race across the wave as it curls up over you.

3 Ride the tube, leading with the front arm and keeping your eyes on the exit, while adjusting your speed to stay in the wave and crouching if necessary to avoid your head being caught by the tube.
4 Keep up speed and, as the wave recedes, shoot out the end onto the shoulder and resume surfing.

There are, of course, many more skills and techniques which can be practised by advanced surfers. Many of these are developments of the basic manoeuvres described in this chapter. It is up to each surfer to develop his or her own portfolio of techniques and manoeuvres which will best display his or her own skills. And it is how those skills are developed that will determine how good a surfer you become.

CHAPTER SEVEN

HOW WEATHER CREATES WAVES

Surfers will sometimes travel long distances in their search for the best waves, yet when they arrive at their destination they often find the waves are disappointing and their journey has been wasted.

One way of avoiding, or at least reducing, such disappointments is to learn how to forecast the weather and, in particular, the wind. Wind creates waves, so by studying the weather you can learn how to predict winds and thus get to know where the best waves might be. You can then head for that part of the coast where surf conditions will be best and get the jump on surfers who don't know how to forecast the weather.

The wind is controlled mostly by pressure systems and learning about pressure systems is dead easy. You only need to be able to read a weather map—issued by the Bureau of Meteorology at regular intervals throughout the day, and published in newspapers as well as being shown on TV—and your chances of finding good waves will increase considerably.

The weather map

The weather map indicates the movement of weather systems on the surface of the earth. The systems are shown as a series of lines in the form of rough circles. These lines, called isobars, indicate pressure gradients just as the contour lines on a topographical map indicate the gradient of hills and mountains: the closer the lines are together, the steeper the gradient and the stronger the winds.

Pressure systems

There are two pressure systems indicated on a weather map: a low—a series of concentric circles, the centre of which is indicated by an 'L'—and a high pressure system, indicated by an 'H'. These move and change shape constantly, hence the changes in the weather from day to day.

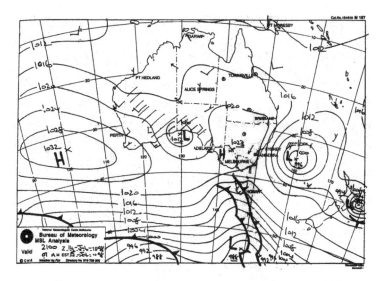

A typical weather map issued by the Bureau of Meteorology showing high and low pressure systems. The low off the south-east coast of New South Wales indicates strong southerly winds blowing along the east coast, building up big swells and thus good surf in that region.

Generally speaking, the low pressure system brings bad weather: strong winds, rain, cloud and sometimes storm conditions. The isobars are usually quite close together; in fact, in a cyclone the circles are so close they almost touch.

The high pressure system brings mostly fine weather: sunny days, light winds and pleasant beach conditions. The lighter winds are indicated by the well spaced out isobars.

As a rule, the best situation for surfing is when there is a low pressure system out to sea, which directs the big swells onto the coast. Cyclones—which are very intense low pressure systems — move down the North Queensland coast and out into the Tasman to bring excellent surf to the beaches of the Gold Coast and northern New South Wales.

In the Southern Hemisphere the wind rotates clockwise around a low pressure and anti-clockwise around a high. The winds follow roughly the path of the isobars, leaning a little inwards on a low and outwards on a high. So by watching a pressure system on a weather map you can determine the direction of the wind and the spacing of the isobars indicates the wind's strength. All weather patterns move around the world from west to east, and if you note the pattern of isobars to the west of your position you will be able to forecast the approaching weather conditions for the next few days. This will enable you to aim for those spots on the coastline where surf conditions are ideal.

AUSTRALIA AND NEW ZEALAND'S TOP SURFING SPOTS

The nature of Australia's coastline means that the best surf is found on the west coast, south coast and parts of the east coast. This is because the swells that create good surf build up in the wide open spaces of the oceans. The west coast faces the Indian Ocean, the south coast faces the Southern Ocean, and the east coast faces the Pacific Ocean. The north coast of the continent is, for the most part, protected from ocean swells by the islands of the Indonesian Archipelago and Papua New Guinea so, even though it is possible for big waves to build up along that coastline in storm and cyclone conditions, they are mostly wind waves. Much the same applies to the northern part of the east coast where the Great Barrier Reef prevents the ocean swells from reaching the coast of north Queensland, between Fraser Island and Cape York.

It's never too soon to start. A young surfer gets the feel of the surf at an early age!

New Zealand lies across the Tasman Sea, opposite to New South Wales, so surfing conditions are much the same. Since New Zealand lies south of Sydney, the climate is usually cooler on the east side of the Tasman. However, that only means a thicker wetsuit should be worn—the waves in the 'Land of the Long White Cloud' can be every bit as exhilarating as those along the east coast of Australia.

Obviously, it is not possible to cover every good surfing spot in this book. For one thing there are too many, and for another surfing spots may change when sandbanks move or the contours of the sea bed change. However, the recognised top spots are covered and providing weather and wave conditions are right, these should offer good surfing most of the year.

A word of warning

Surfing spots can produce dangerous surf in certain conditions. If you are an expert and experienced at surfing in most conditions, you will know how to judge the waves and determine whether or not you can handle them. If you are a beginner or have not experienced big sea conditions in unfamiliar waters, then take care. There are all sorts of dangers that can lie in wait for the reckless surfer, from unknown and dangerous rips to reefs that lie only centimetres beneath the surface when the wave sucks back. Be sensible, mature and cautious in your approach to unfamiliar waters and you will survive and enjoy your surfing. If you are reckless and stupid you might wind up in a local hospital or a wheelchair, and that may mean the end of your surfing! Take time to study the waves and watch what local surfers do before you paddle out. Even better, talk to some of the locals and suss out the problem areas. And never, never surf alone.

Australia

The west coast

From North West Cape and the town of Exmouth at the northern end of the west coast to Carnarvon the coastline is very rugged and access to the surf is limited, so travelling to the far north of the west coast is not a very practical proposition. Probably the northernmost surfing spot of any consequence is at **Red Bluff**, about 130 kilometres north of Carnarvon. This area has very demanding surf which breaks over a coral and rock bottom, and should only be tackled if you are an experienced and competent surfer.

Access to the surf outside of Shark Bay can also be difficult as there are sheer cliffs dropping into the sea on the west face of Dirk Hartog Island and the coastline immediately to the south known as the Zuytdorp Coast. Between Kalbarri and Port Gregory there are a number of good surfing spots and access is not too difficult although a four-wheel drive may be necessary in some places. **Jakes Point** is one of the most popular places while near the town of Kalbarri **Blue Hole** and the break off the harbour entrance are known to provide good waves. South from Port Gregory to Geraldton there are again some good surf spots but most are difficult to get to without a four-wheel drive and local knowledge.

Just north of Geraldton is a popular spot called **Coronation**, while in Geraldton itself good waves can be found in a number of spots, particularly around **Point Moore**. South, towards Dongara, there is a good spot at **Flat Rocks** and a popular break lies at a place known as **Headbutts**, but access to these may be difficult without a four-wheel drive. South from Dongara there is little surf because the ocean swell is broken by the continuous offshore reef that runs right down the coast here. Indeed, this situation continues down the coastline past Perth and, although some waves will be found when swell conditions are high, for the most part good surf on this stretch of coastline is fairly sparse.

The offshore reefs block the ocean swell from most of the beaches at Perth and south to Bunbury, so surf is mostly small along this stretch of coastline. However, the surf that is to be found on the beaches and headlands south from Cape Naturaliste is a different story altogether. Here the offshore reefs disappear and the coastline is subjected to the full fury of the Southern Ocean and Indian Ocean swells. The surfing here is legendary.

Almost anywhere down this stretch of coastline you will find good surfing spots. Here are the classic breaks such as **Margaret River** and **Yallingup**, locations where world-class surfing contests are held because the surf is so powerful and consistent. The road along the coast runs from Cape Naturaliste to Cape Leeuwin on the south-west corner of the continent and access to the numerous surfing spots is fairly easy. There are too many to list in detail; the whole region is a surfer's paradise. **Margaret River** is the focal point and most of the popular spots lie to the north of this famous place. **Boranup Beach** is probably the southernmost spot with reasonable access and good waves.

The west coast.

The south coast

Across the southern coast of Western Australia are superb beaches that can offer good surfing conditions, but they are not reliable as they face the mighty Southern Ocean. When the Antarctic gales that race around the world in southern latitudes—the Roaring Forties—send swells onto this coastline the waves are usually huge but can be too blown about for good surfing. Access to the surf along this stretch can also be difficult in places, although some good breaks can be reached if you get to know your way around. **Muttonbird Beach** is the most popular spot west of Albany as is **Cheyne Beach** to the east; otherwise there is only average surfing in and around the town of Albany.

The south coast off the port of Esperance has a barrier of islands—the Recherche Archipelago—which blocks the oncoming swells and reduces the surfing potential of the otherwise great

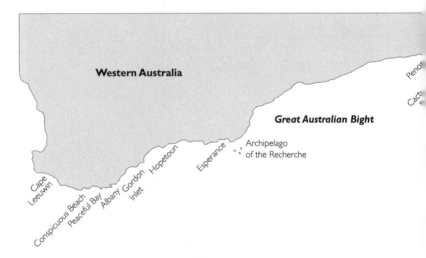

The south coast.

beaches. From this point onwards access to the coastline by road can become difficult, except for four-wheel drives. Most surfers bypass this stretch of the Great Australian Bight and head across the Nullarbor for Ceduna.

Just before Ceduna is the township of Penong and close by lies one of the legendary surfing spots along the South Australian coast—**Point Sinclair**. Among the many fine breaks in this area are **Cactus** and **Witzigs** and access is generally easy. Apart from its reputation as a fine surfing spot, the coastline here is renowned as a haven for white pointer sharks!

The coastline around the Eyre Peninsula also has some rugged surfing spots as here the land projects down into the raging Southern Ocean. Big swells, rugged headlands and occasional windswept beaches make up the geography of this coast. The action is almost all on the western side of the peninsula with

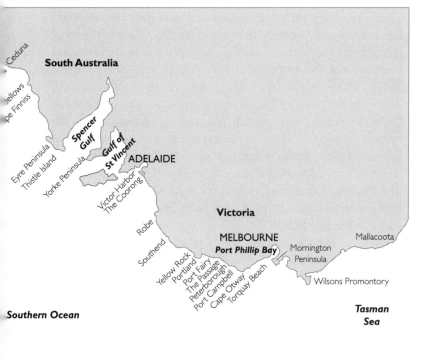

Elliston the main access point. **Cape Finniss** and adjacent **Blackfellows** are two well-known spots on this stretch, but care is needed as the breaks here are rugged and the limestone rocks under the surface can inflict serious injury if you wipeout. There is not much offering around the southern tip of the cape and into Spencer Gulf although some surfers claim **Thistle Island** provides good surfing if you can get out to it.

Spencer Gulf and the Gulf of St Vincent are both sheltered waterways with little or no surf, but the southern tip of the **Yorke Peninsula** is a popular spot with local surfers. South of Adelaide the old port of Victor Harbor has a few good surfing spots along the nearby coastline, but to the east long unbroken stretches of beach disappear over the horizon towards the border with Victoria. On some of these beaches, notably the **Coorong**, good waves can be found depending on the offshore banks, and near the towns of Robe and South End there are a number of bays and headlands which turn on good surf when conditions are right.

The south-west coast of Victoria is akin to the Margaret River coast of Western Australia in terms of surfing. Some of the most recognised names in the surfing calendar are located between Portland and the entrance to Port Phillip Bay—notably **Bell's Beach**, where world-class surfing contests are held each year. There are too many to describe here; surfing is part of the scene along this entire coastal stretch, but working eastwards from the town of Portland the most significant surfing beaches would be as follows: **Yellow Rock**, which lies near Portland; **The Passage**, south of Port Fairy; **Massacres**, off Peterborough, also known as **The Elevator**; **Easter Reef**, near Port Campbell; **Johanna**, situated to the west of Cape Otway; **Lorne**; **Bell's Beach**; **Winki Pop**; **Jan Juc**; and **Torquay Beach**.

On the eastern side of Port Phillip Bay the Mornington Peninsula offers a few good surfing spots, notably **Gunnamatta** and **The Pines**, with **Corsair** a popular break right at the entrance to Port Phillip Bay. Phillip Island is renowned for its fine beach break at **Woolamai Beach** and reef break at **Express Point**.

Lennox Head has good point breaks on the east coast, but getting out can be tricky.

Even further east along the coast towards Wilsons Promontory are numerous bays and headlands where surf may be found, but there is nothing of significance and access, especially on the Promontory, is only by foot through the bush. Much of the coastline between Wilsons Promontory and the NSW border consists of long beaches, all of which have potential to offer a few surfable breaks under the right conditions. The coastline becomes more rugged as it turns the corner near the NSW border and there are a few breaks on the headlands near Mallacoota.

The east coast

Through the Ben Boyd National Park, south of Eden, you can reach a popular break known as **Saltwater**, the first of the good surfing spots on the NSW coast. **Pambula Rivermouth**, to the north, is well known for its barrels and is just across the bay from the **Merimbula Bar**, equally famous for its barrels when the swells are up. The coastline north from this area consists of a series of small inlets and bays with rocky headlands in between, and it is littered with surfing spots, ranging from beginner's level to good breaks that, in the right conditions, can provide top surf. **Narooma Breakwater** is one of these, as is **Moruya Breakwall**.

Beaches on the New South Wales south coast offer great surfing when the swell is running. Some of the better known spots near Ulladulla are **Golf Course Reef**, the **Ulladulla Bommie** and **Potholes**. Just to the north is popular **Green Island** with its good left-hander. **Black Rock** lies on the southern side of the Jervis Bay promontory and is a spot much loved by Sydney surfers. North of Jervis Bay reefs, bays and headlands provide good surf in most places. **Kiama** has some good beaches and **Bass Point** is also a popular spot. From Wollongong to Sydney the beaches all provide surf in the right swell conditions. **Sandon Point**, just north of the 'Gong, has a fine point break while **Stanwell Park** and **Garie Beach** are also popular surfing spots.

Sydney's beaches need no introduction to surfers who have visited the city. Every beach has good surfing potential and many world-champion surfers, both past and present, have developed their skills in the waves off these beaches. It would be impossible to describe every break but the more notable, working from the south, would be **Shark Island** and **Cronulla Point** at Cronulla; **Maroubra Beach** and **Lurline Bay** are good spots on the south side as, of course, is the famous **Bondi Beach**. On the north side, **Manly Beach** is the home of many international surfers; and the many indented beaches that stretch away to the north are all surf beaches with great reputations, probably the best known being **North Narrabeen**, where international contests are held regularly.

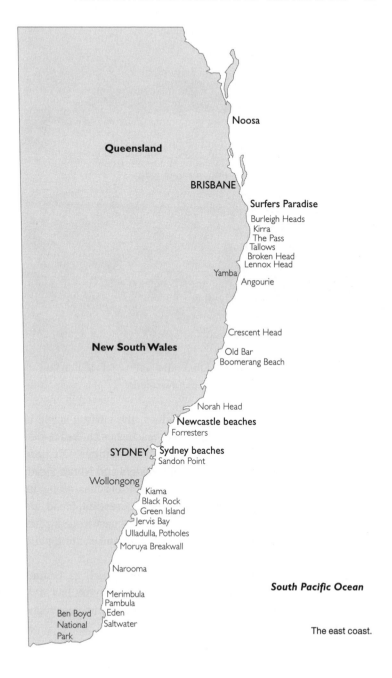

Noosa

Queensland

BRISBANE

Surfers Paradise

Burleigh Heads
Kirra
The Pass
Tallows
Broken Head
Lennox Head
Yamba
Angourie

Crescent Head

Old Bar
Boomerang Beach

New South Wales

Norah Head
Newcastle beaches
Forresters

SYDNEY Sydney beaches
Sandon Point

Wollongong
Kiama
Black Rock
Green Island
Jervis Bay
Ulladulla, Potholes
Moruya Breakwall

Narooma

South Pacific Ocean

Merimbula
Pambula
Ben Boyd   Eden
National   Saltwater
Park

The east coast.

Boomerang Beach—a favourite surfing spot on the east coast.

On the Central Coast, north of Sydney, the surfing scene is much the same: indented bays and beaches with headlands between offering good surfing under most conditions. Offshore reefs make for outstanding breaks at **Forresters** and **Norah Head**, while Newcastle has its share of good surf beaches along its seaboard. **Boomerang Beach**, **Old Bar** and **Crescent Head** are known as good surfing spots on the mid-north coast while farther north, near Yamba, **Angourie** has a well-known and exciting point break as well as a very pretty little bay.

The north coast provides legendary names such as **Lennox Head**, **Broken Head**, **Tallows**, **The Pass**, all in the Byron Bay area. Farther north and into Queensland the names continue: **Kirra**, **Burleigh**, **Surfers** and **Noosa**.

Bass Strait

Trial Harbour · Zeehan

Tasmania

HOBART

Eaglehawk Neck

Tasman Peninsula

Bruny Island

Southern Ocean

Tasman Sea

The Tasmanian coast.

Tasmania

There are a number of factors that limit surfing in Tasmania, despite the fact that some of the biggest seas around Australia roll onto its western shores. Firstly, the island state is the part of Australia closest to the Antarctic so the water is several degrees colder than on the mainland. Secondly, the west coast—where the big waves are located—is mostly inaccessible by land as much of it is wilderness. There is access to the north-west tip and a good break can be found at **Trial Harbour**, near Zeeahan, but otherwise the overland approach to the coast is pretty tough going. The north coast faces onto Bass Strait, which inhibits the size of ocean swells and, while there are a few spots worth surfing, there is generally not much on offer.

The east coast is the main area for any kind of water sports. Access is mostly good, the water is clean and the beaches superb. There are some good surfing spots all along this coast, although none are really outstanding or consistent. The **Tasman Peninsula** offers the best prospects with good breaks at **Eaglehawk Neck**. Also **Bruny Island** can offer pleasant surfing when the swell is moving up from the south.

New Zealand

North Island—west coast

The North Island is the most popular for surfing, probably because of the colder water to the south. From the tip of Northland the west coast runs south-east in a long stretch known as **Ninety Mile Beach** and, as with any long beach, good surf can be found here, depending on the banks. However, the best spot to find good waves is **Shipwreck Bay** in the southern corner.

Farther south on the west coast the popular beaches of **Muriwai** and **Piha** provide reasonable surf close to the city of Auckland, although perhaps the best known of these west coast beaches is **Raglan**, with one of the best point breaks in New Zealand. Access is easy from Hamilton and there are a number of good surfing spots all along this coast.

Beaches on the west coast port of **New Plymouth** offer good surfing when there are waves. **Kumera** is considered one of the best spots in the area and is well known for its long left-hand break, which can run for 100 metres or more. There are other good breaks along this coastline and access is gained along the coast road which runs through **Okato** and **Opunake**.

North Island—east coast

From the northern tip of the North Island, there are numerous spots where surfers will find waves, one of the best being **Taronui Bay** where good breaks are sometimes over shallow reefs. **Sandy Bay**, a little farther south, is a popular surfing sport and competitions are often held here; access is easy through Whangarei. A little to the south again, **Goat Island** produces good surf in a big swell as does **Great Barrier Island** although access to these beaches means either a flight or a ferry trip to the island and some means of transport once there.

The Coromandel Peninsula is a scenically delightful region that can produce good surf in some spots. The two most popular areas are **Tairua** and **Whangamata**, the latter being best known for

The New Zealand coast.

its bar break. From the east coast town of **Gisborne**, good waves can often be found in the immediate vicinity. **Makorori** is is considered one of the best, while there can be some good breaks on **The Island**. Where the coast cuts into Hawkes Bay, the headland known as **Mahia Peninsula** provides some of the best surfing on the east coast and, although rather isolated, it has reasonable access from Wairoa or Gisborne.

Hawkes Bay is known more for its black sand beaches, but there are a few spots where waves can be found, especially to the south of the town. Of these, **Waimarama** and **Cray Bay** probably offers the best variety.

The coast south of Wellington to Hawkes Bay has a great range of surf, although access to most of the areas is limited. Through Martinborough there is access to the big waves at **Tora** and **White Rock**. When the surf is running some of the biggest waves in New Zealand can be found here.

South Island

Surfing is perhaps not as popular on the South Island as on the North Island, due to the climate. This is particularly the case on the west coast, where the conditions are not dissimilar to those on the west coast of Tasmania. Battered by the Roaring Forties gales, the coastline has huge swells but these are usually so blown about and icy cold that even the most intrepid surfer shuns the area.

The east coast has a few spots where brave souls in thick wetsuits can find waves. Probably one of the most popular is **Kaikoura**, well to the north and where the water is not too cold. The **Otago Peninsula** has many good surf spots in its small bays, with easy access from Dunedin. However, there are two factors which inhibit surfing at Otago: the temperature of the water and big sharks. Like Spencer Gulf in South Australia, the waters off the Otago Peninsula are home to the white pointer and there have been fatalities among surfers in this area.

INDEX